Your Feelings Matter!

For more information about our books, including printable handouts, please visit our website at www.harbourholmespublishing.com. For permission requests, please e-mail harbourholmespublishing@gmail.com.

ISBN: 978-1-09832-860-3

Your Feelings Matter!

A Story for Children Who Have Witnessed Domestic Violence

Amber Holmes LCSW

Tiffany Sanders LCSW, LISW-CP

Illustrated by Maru Guevara

HARBOUR & HOLMES PUBLISHING • CHARLOTTE, NC

DEDICATION

Your Feelings Matter! is dedicated to children exposed to domestic violence all over the world

My name is Riley and I am seven years old. I live with my Mommy and her boyfriend in our house. They have been together for a long time. Mommy really likes him, and I do too.

When Mommy first met her boyfriend, things were great. He was nice to Mommy and me. We did fun things like play board games, watch movies, and go to the park!

But today things changed...

After school, I had a soccer game. I scored a goal and the ball made a *whoosh* sound as it went into the net. Mommy and her boyfriend cheered me on, and I was excited.

Following my soccer game, we went to my favorite pizza place. Yummy! I love game days because we always have pizza!

Before bedtime, as I was brushing my teeth, I could hear Mommy's boyfriend yelling and screaming at Mommy. He sounded like he was mad, like really mad.

I peeked down the hallway to see what was happening and I saw Mommy's boyfriend push her and hit her in the face. I slipped back into the bathroom and felt very afraid. My body was shaking, and I started to cry. I felt confused. How could this be happening?

Mommy went into her bedroom and called 911. The police officers came to help. The tall police officer wrote things down in a little notebook as Mommy spoke. Then they took Mommy's boyfriend away in the police car. I did not know how to feel. I love Mommy's boyfriend, but I was angry and sad that he had hurt Mommy.

The next day, Mommy was sad and crying a lot. That made me feel sad. At dinnertime, Mommy was quiet, but I did not feel like talking either. I pushed my broccoli around the plate with my fork. I missed Mommy's boyfriend. Is he coming back? Does he love Mommy and me? Did I do something wrong?

When I went to school the next day, I had a hard time paying attention to my teacher. My tummy was hurting, my leg was shaking, and I could not stop thinking about what happened. The thoughts kept circling around my head like a silly dog chasing his tail.

I did not want to play with my friends at recess. My teacher noticed something was different and asked me, "Are you okay?" I started to cry, and I could not talk. She told me she wanted me to speak with the School Social Worker, Mrs. Brown.

Mrs. Brown came out to the playground and walked me to her office. At first, I thought I was in trouble, but Mrs. Brown told me she was only there to help. She said sometimes she needs help too.

I decided to tell Mrs. Brown about Mommy's boyfriend. I told her about how he hit Mommy. I told her I was scared, and worried Mommy's boyfriend was going to hurt her again. Mrs. Brown told me it is normal to feel what I was feeling. She even told me that our bodies give us "weird" feelings when things are not right.

Mrs. Brown told me we were going to play the *Body Wand* game to figure out where I was having "weird" feelings. She told me to make a beeping noise when she passed the spot that did not feel right. She scanned me from the top of my head to the tip of my toes.

When the *Body Wand* passed my head, heart, and tummy, I made the beeping sound.

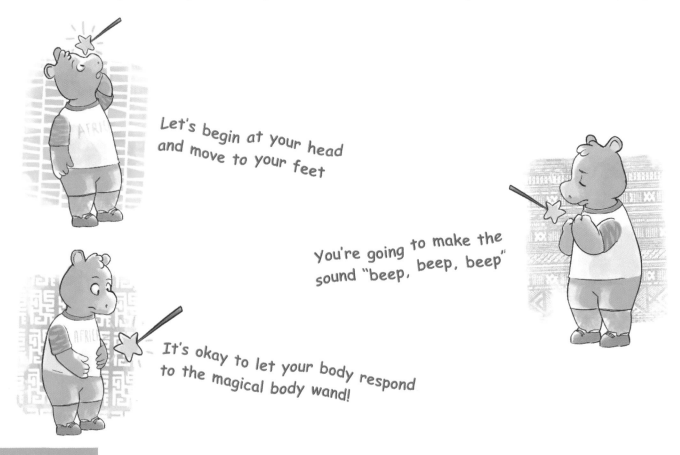

Let's begin at your head and move to your feet

You're going to make the sound "beep, beep, beep"

It's okay to let your body respond to the magical body wand!

Give it a try!

Use a pen/pencil or any object as a wand. Move the wand slowly from head to toe. Encourage the child to make the beeping noise where they have a weird feeling. **Note to Adult:** Always assess the comfort level of the child. **

Mrs. Brown told me it is normal to have an upset tummy, a dizzy head, or a fast beating heart when stressful things are happening at home. She also told me that I am in control of my body. She said there are lots of things I can do to help my body feel better. Then she told me we were going to practice the *Breathing Buddy* and to follow her lead.

BREATHE IN

If your body feels weird and you want to shout

Your Breathing Buddy helps you breathe in and out

BREATHE OUT

Then your body will start to slow down

And you'll feel calmer all around!

Give it a try!

Demonstrate for the child a breathing technique with a funny twist (i.e. breathe in through your nose raising your arms like you are a balloon blowing up, slowly release your breath deflating your balloon putting your arms back to your side). Prompt the child to mimic your movements - repeat three times. Then, encourage the child to create their own movements for you to mimic - repeat three times.

Flap
Your wings and fly like a toucan in a circle.

Hop
From rock to rock like a tiger 15 times.

Stomp
Like a bear for 60 seconds.

Run
In place as fast as you can like a cheetah for 30 seconds.

Leap
Like a frog ten times.

Sway
Your arms like an elephant's trunk back and forth 5 times.

Chomp
Your hands like a crocodile 5 times.

Jump
In and out of a river like a fish 15 times.

Give it a try!

Direct the child in some exercise movements imitating animals. Use illustration above as a guide.

Spinning head and tingling toes
Pounding hearts and sniffling nose

After we played *Breathing Buddy*, my body started to feel a little better. Mrs. Brown told me there were other ways to control my weird feelings and better deal with my thoughts. She called it grounding.

Grounding can help our bodies calm down even more. She told me we were going to play the *Moving Jungle* to bring my mind and body back to the present moment.

Feelings, feelings all over the place
Feelings, feelings let's slow down our pace

My body felt calmer after pretending to be animals in the jungle. Mrs. Brown told me we would also talk about some of my other feelings, like being sad, afraid, and confused. She said this was called *Talk Time* and I could talk about big or little things.

It's always good to talk about how you're feeling
Because it helps everyone with healing

Letting your emotions out is the key
Speak your words and set yourself free!

She told me to always state what I am feeling and why I am feeling that way. She told me to use the format "who (I am), what (feeling), and why (because)." We started to practice how to talk to Mommy about my feelings. She said it is better to talk because holding in my feelings would be like a volcano ready to explode. She pretended to be Mommy and I practiced talking about my feelings.

Give it a try!

Help the child use the format "I am feeling _____ because_____." Encourage the usage of both sad and happy emotions for this exercise.

When I got home from school, I told Mommy about all the things Mrs. Brown and I did together. The *Body Wand* game...the *Breathing Buddy*... the *Moving Jungle*... and *Talk Time*. Mommy said Mrs. Brown called her this morning and they will be meeting tomorrow. I am happy Mommy gets to talk with Mrs. Brown too because she is a very nice lady.

The next day, Mommy came to the school to meet with Mrs. Brown and I. Mrs. Brown helped us make a safety plan for moving forward. We talked about finding a safe place in my house for me to run to if Mommy's boyfriend comes back and tries to hurt Mommy again. We also talked about how it is okay to call 911 and that I should learn my address to tell the 911 operator.

After the meeting, we went to get ice cream. Mommy told me she was proud of me for talking with Mrs. Brown and learning how to be in control of my body and express my feelings. That made me smile!

I took a deep breath and finally told Mommy how I felt about all that had happened. I told her I missed her boyfriend, but I did not like that he was mean to her. I told her I was scared when he hit her and confused about where he is now.

Your Feelings matter!

Mommy looked down at me and kissed me on the forehead and said, "Riley, thank you for letting me know how you feel because *Your Feelings Matter*. I am working to make sure I am doing what is best for us."

She also said it is okay for me to worry sometimes but it is her job to keep me safe. With the help of Mrs. Brown and the police officers, Mommy said we had a safety plan in place. I gave Mommy a big, tight hug.

I know things will not all change tomorrow, but Mommy and I are moving forward. Most importantly, I learned my feelings matter. Guess what? **Yours do too!**

A Note to Parents and Caregivers:

Children are often the silent victims of Domestic Violence and can be impacted emotionally, mentally, and physically. Domestic Violence is an individualized experience and looks different for each child. Being a witness to Domestic Violence can include **SEEING** actual incidents of abuse, **HEARING** threats or fighting noises from another room in the residence, **OBSERVING** the aftermath of physical abuse (such as blood, bruises, tears, torn clothing, or broken items) and **AWARENESS** of the tension in the home. When children can talk about their feelings with caring adults, it can decrease negative consequences both short-term and long-term.

Guiding Questions: The purpose of the guiding questions is to build rapport with the child. It will also create a comfortable environment, normalize their experience, and provide an assessment of the child's thoughts on the topic.

- Where is your favorite place to eat? (page 3)
- Think about a time you were at your favorite place. What did you see? What did you hear? What did you touch? What did you taste? What did you smell? (page 3)
- Is it okay for Riley to have those feelings about Mommy's boyfriend? (page 5)
- Why do you think Riley misses Mommy's boyfriend? (page 6)
- Do you think Riley missing Mommy's boyfriend is okay? Why or why not? (page 6)
- Do you have someone like Mrs. Brown at your school? (page 8)
- Who is an adult you can trust at your school? (page 8)
- How do you think Riley felt when he told Mrs. Brown what happened at home? Why? (page 9)
- Where else do you think the body can feel weird? (page 10)
- Did you know the body tells you when something is not right? (page 10)
- Can you tell me a time when your body felt weird? (page 10)
- Which was your favorite animal exercise? (page 12)
- What else do you think Riley and Mommy put in their safety plan? (page 16)
- Where do you think Riley and Mommy went to be safe? Where do you feel safe? Who makes you feel safe? (page 18)
- Is there anyone who does not make you feel safe? (page 18)

ABOUT THE AUTHORS

Amber Holmes, LCSW is a Licensed Clinical Social Worker and Professional Coach based in NC. With a passion for working with children, families, and adolescents, Amber started her trauma focused work in an intensive in-home setting. Today, Amber works for her local county in partnership with the police department, responding to incidents involving child victims or witnesses exposed to traumatic events. Amber is trained in Cognitive Behavioral Therapy and continues to enhance her knowledge and therapeutic skills with the latest evidenced based findings centered around trauma. Amber enjoys spending time with her husband, being a foodie, traveling, and nature adventures.

Tiffany Sanders LCSW, LISW-CP is a Licensed Social Worker in North Carolina and South Carolina. Tiffany has extensive experience working with traumatized children and their families. She is professionally trained in trauma focused modalities and treatment approaches including the Neurosequential Model of Therapeutics (NMT), Child and Family Traumatic Stress Intervention (CFTSI) and Trauma Focused Cognitive Behavioral Therapy (TF-CBT). Tiffany currently works full-time as a clinician with her local government to aid the local police department with providing therapeutic support to children exposed traumatizing events. Tiffany currently lives in North Carolina, where she e reading, photography, and traveling.